Symptoms of a Teratoma

Symptoms of a Teratoma

Matthew O'Leary

Library of Congress Number: 2017910418

ISBN: 978-1-942081-13-5

"Psittacosis" and "Kwashiorkor" previously appeared in *Fall Lines – a literary convergence,* vol. III.

Contents

To my supernova, and all the remaining stars in my sky.

Prologue

One of the most basic biological instincts is that of self-preservation. If you hear a noise, you react. If you feel pain, you pull back from it. This is how nature keeps us alive. The more cynical among us suggest that even an act that seems selfless, like protecting your children before yourself, is still ultimately an act of self-preservation. Instinctively, you protect your genetics.

But the world is full of chaos, and even genetics fall prey to mutations. Sometimes, the mutation is physical, a mass of cells growing in the wrong place, killing its host. Other times, the mutation involves neurological pathways and affects the brain. The brain begins to have the wrong thoughts. These thoughts can kill the host just as easily as any tumor.

This is a biopsy of my mutation. It's a mutation passed down from generation to generation. My grandfather carried it with him into the Battle of Okinawa, where it gained strength and made him into a person he didn't deserve to be. My mother inherited it, and it followed her into adulthood, never fully known to me until a different mutation took her away.

The past few years have been good for my mutation. It's gained strength and confidence, while sapping mine away. The pieces that follow are my attempt to fight back. Maybe if I show it to the world, ugly and deformed, perhaps it will become the one afraid to show its face. Maybe I'll take my confidence back. Maybe I'll remember what it is to want to preserve myself. I want to tell it, "you may still kill me, but you've got a lot more work to do."

Cancer of the Lung

He closes his eyes and inhales. On the exhale, he counts down from ten. He runs out of air around four, which is when he opens his eyes again. The tension hasn't gone anywhere. His hands still shake, the dryness in his throat persists.

Out of the corner of his eye, the hands on the clock shift one minute, backwards.

"You can't smoke in here."

He doesn't respond, even when she starts clearing her throat in his direction. Instead, he looks down at her foot, wearing a pink pump, tapping impatiently. The rhythm matches a Rolling Stones song whose tune he vaguely remembers.

"Hey!" He lifts his face to meet the woman's. She snorts in disgust. "Didn't you hear me? No smoking!"

He looks at his hands, the fingers yellow with nicotine stains. "I don't have a cigarette."

"Don't lie to me," she screams. She stomps her pump, connecting squarely with the toes of his loafers.

"Shit!" He pulls his foot back, and tucks it underneath the chair. "What the hell is wrong with you?"

The woman tosses her head back and laughs. "You think that hurts? Just wait! It's all downhill from here." She grips her purse so tightly her pointed nails press into her palm, and the sharp points of the painted acrylic penetrate the flesh. Tiny trenches fill and drain. Blood drips from between her white knuckles. It falls to the carpet, soaks into the fibers, spreads like a bouquet of blossoming flowers.

"Sir?"

The man looks up towards the voice from the window. The receptionist tilts her head to the left, and the man realizes she is simply mimicking his own unconscious tilt.

The woman has disappeared. The stain remains.

"Are you okay, sir?"

"Y-yeah," he stammers, and rubs his temples. As the receptionist nods and turns to a stack of papers, he raises his hand to get her attention.

The receptionist chuckles. "You're not in school, sir. Do you have a question?"

"How much longer until he sees me?"

"It shouldn't be much longer. When I last saw him, he was looking over your x-rays."

"And how did they look?"

Her smile falters. "I don't have any medical training, sir."

He runs his hands through the thickness of his hair. "Still, you see this sort of thing every day. I'm sure you have a pretty informed opinion."

Her friendly demeanor becomes stern, gravely serious. "Sir, I cannot discuss any aspect of your treatment, sir." Her last word, bizarrely said twice, hangs in the air awkwardly, and she turns back to her papers. His glance falls downward to the stain: drying, turning black. With each breath, the mass lifts and falls.

The doctor calls his name, and he doesn't hear it. The call blurs into white noise. He closes his eyes and inhales. On the exhale, he counts down from ten. He runs out of air around six, which is when he opens his eyes again.

Two seconds later, the stain inhales.

Tuberculosis

"Chopin coughs with infinite grace." He joined Chekhov, Browning, Poe, Bronte. Artists the world over coughed blood and infected lung fluids onto the greatest artistic works of all time. Lord Byron wrote it in a love letter, but was uncharacteristically rejected. Instead, he was courted by unsanitary surgical instruments. They sliced him strategically to let him bleed back to life, and he died of sepsis, every organ screaming.

The Doctor's favorite book is *The Seagull.* He has a license to carry a firearm, which he shows me, tucked inside his sports coat.

The once honorary disease of gothic artists is now the lesser of the banes of the African continent. Children die before they get the chance to write *Jane Eyre* or *The Cask of Amontillado*. In Swaziland, the age expectancy is fifty years. Eighty-three percent have tuberculosis and AIDS. AIDS kills faster. The national motto of Swaziland is "Siyinqaba." In Swazi, it means "we hide ourselves away."

The Doctor slides a needle beneath my skin. The skin bubbles like a blister, and I wonder if I could slap the mound and splash the tuberculin all over my arm. The Doctor reads my mind, warns me of a false positive. "No scratching, no itching, no touching."

He pulls the gun from its holster and holds it under my nose. It smells like sweat. I scream "For the love of God, Montressor!" When he pulls the trigger, the gun clicks. We both look at it in disbelief.

"Which act is this?"

"The second, I think."

He nods thoughtfully, puts the gun away.

When I was an EMT, my partner and I spent ten minutes in a patient's filthy house before we found out that she had TB. Our dispatchers either didn't know, or didn't feel it was important to tell us. Being younger and less experienced, my mind immediately went towards leaping off of her couch, knocking down whoever I had to in an attempt to get to the door. The more pragmatic side of me recognized that if I was exposed, it was already too late. A few years later, I had that bubble blown into my arm for a position at a rehabilitation facility. Everything came back clean. Three months later, they fired me for leaning against the physical therapist's parallel bars. It was the first time in my life I cried upon losing a job. It was also the first time I'd seen a corpse outside of a funeral. Now I've seen plenty.

With a deafening bang, the Doctor's gun goes off. The bullet tears through his leather belt and gets lodged in the chair. When he stands up, his pants fall down, and we all have a good laugh. End scene.

Aphasia*

On the television is the red-faced man who can't stop talking, and every word out of his mouth is condescending and venal. Each syllable rubs me raw. He's telling a story about a child, living in South America. When she was ten years old, her stepfather raped her. The authorities, steeped in the savage conservatism of the Roman Catholic Church, forced her to carry the child to term. The flushed gentleman on the screen couldn't be happier.

Only a fraction of a percent of our genetic material separates one human being from another, and I find myself ashamed of the biology I share with this man. Words fail, and the mind retreats to erasure. I contemplate ripping my tongue from the muscle, pushing it down the lumen of my digestive tract, letting it dissolve with my imaginary ulcers. Like a phantom limb, I taste the bile, a precursor to a vomitus that never comes.

Leo hangs in the center of the sky, between my mother and myself. The lion is dominated by a regent some eighty light years from the Earth. If he dies today, the little girl can watch him burn out on her deathbed, her elderly child by her side. I hope she never hears what that man on the television said about her, and that his words will be forgotten in those eighty years. From where she lays, he is long dead, a historic tribute to 21st century depravity. When the anchors announce it, I turn off the television, suppressing a smile. I work to reach into my own humanity, seeking some semblance of sympathy with his family, but despite my best efforts, I remember the words he was so eager to share. They lay him to rest in his bed, surrounded by his unique flavor of venom.

I take in other faces, while standing in line. The bank's televisions show his funeral without sound, and I'm the only one watching. On the screen, the mourners wail in silence. The station breaks for commercial.

Psittacosis*

"This way to sexy bird antics!" reads the sign after my twelfth hour on the road. I couldn't beat the sun into the Empire State much less your precious Salt City. I had to stop for a cuttlebone and coffee at Tim Horton's. You're so thankful that dinner is already on the table, sesame seeds without all that filler they sell at the big box stores. You go to work and I start looking around.

It's been over a year now, but it feels like no time at all. You added an obscene number of Audubon prints. I point out the Carolina parakeet, one of the South's most beautiful birds, extinct for a century. They died out because they had a bad habit of returning to unsafe areas. When a hunter shot one, the rest of the flock would go to investigate. I have no idea what that must be like, coming back again and again, knowing I'll be shot down. Shells and bullets may break my bones, but words will leave the deepest wounds. Did I mention you live in the Salt City?

My lungs are getting spotty with dust, and my eyes have glazed over. In three days, you'll fly again, southwest for the summer, back to Tornado Alley to really test your wings. We learned that you were a seabird, and we spent an entire year flying together over the ocean. When I practiced dying, you lit on my back. You pecked at me until I took you to breakfast. We drank coffee across the longest table in the world, and I watched where my feet went. We always went in different directions. Maybe we always will.

The Doctor gives me the side-eye when I ask him, "is this avian flu?"

"Where do you think you are, China?" I mumble something about racism under my breath, and he pretends not to hear me. "It's a hotbed for disease over there. You remember SARS?"

I remember SARS.

"First person to get it during the outbreak was a patient with an atypical pneumonia. He gave it to his doctor." He lowers his clipboard and glares at me.

"I-I-I-" I stammer, but he cuts me off.

"You don't have SARS. You don't have avian flu. You don't have H1N1. You'll get that when pigs fly." He starts laughing uncontrollably, and someone bangs on the wall from the neighboring examination room.

He tears a page from his prescription pad, which he had somehow filled while he was laughing. "You know the United States government wanted to use it as a biological weapon. They suspended the program."

"Doxycycline."

"I guess they thought chemical warfare was for the birds." He grins, all teeth. It's funny, but for some reason, I can't laugh.

Couvade Syndrome*

Every man can remember the day he has to buy his first bra. I had just taken my shirt off to take a shower, when my wife noticed how much I had blossomed. "I need to find some larger dresses, anyway." I could tell that she was jealous. While both of us were growing into a new cup size, mine were supple, perky, and unencumbered by gravity. I could still turn the boys' heads.

I'm sitting on the couch, writing Fibonacci numbers on my legs in lip pencil. On the screen is an Australian domestic drama about being alienated from your parents. My swollen wife comes in. "Scoot over. I want to shoot some zombies." The seventeenth number is the first to have four digits. A zombie's head bursts like a blister. I can feel the child moving inside of me. I hope the delivery is easy.

Between scorched earth and harvest moon, I find time for breathing. The romantic comedies make it a mantra of pursed lips and comic gasping. My wife hands me a bottle of beer and tells me to drink, but I refuse. I've read too many journals, seen too many pictures of small heads, smooth philtrums, what doctors call a thin vermillion. Vermillion, I say, feeling the word between breaths. Maybe if it's a girl. What if it's a boy? My wife suggests Hypochondria. Not a fan.

She insists on using her own Doctor. Hers is a woman, so I naturally worry about her ability to empathize with my problems. She refuses to meet my gaze when she asks me important questions. "How far apart are the contractions? Are you going to want an epidural?" I don't have a watch, and they won't let me turn on my cellphone, so I have no idea what time it is. And I want to have a natural birth. I don't trust the fog of drugs, plus, I have a particularly sensitive spinal cord. Last week, I ate some peanut butter, and my spinal cord was itching all day. The Female Doctor looks at me with the same expression that my wife has given me for the last nine months. It emanates warmth and concern.

My child is a boy. Through the glass, I can see him squirm under his blue blanket. His mother was only allowed to hold him for a few minutes, before they returned him to his sterile plastic drawer. On the big white label, his name is misspelled. I get the nurse's attention, and point at the child. She flashes a smile that immediately disappears. It doesn't matter. I'll be the next one to hold him. It's never too early to teach him to be a man.

Kwashiorkor*

I stand in front of the mirror, stripped to my underwear. The pot belly that I had spent my whole life dreading had been there for some time, but the past few months had added the vivid red tiger stripes that one usually heard about among women discussing pregnancy. It started with the "freshman fifteen," the characteristic weight gain seen by college students first breaking away from their parents' meal plans. It fluctuated back and forth until I lost my job, when I was caught crying in the break room over her pancreas. Taking care of myself fell by the wayside. They found no stones, so what did it matter if I ate too many carbs?

In Sub-Saharan Africa, a teenager looks at his emaciated reflection in a mudpuddle. His eyes are sallow, his belly distended from lack of protein. His liver is enlarged, carrying more fat than the rest of his body. He can't quite put his finger on what has him down. Disease is rampant, he hasn't eaten in days, and his younger sister was raped by members of a local rebel group who sometimes terrorize them with assault rifles and machetes. But inside he feels somewhat unsettled, as if in some far corner of the world, a middle-class white man is self-conscious of his appearance. The teenager wishes he weren't suffering from extreme dehydration, so he could cry the appropriate tears. He lies down and reflects on his partner in suffering.

When I refresh my Facebook page for the second time in a minute, a story pops up. "Children are dying in Africa." I share it without clicking the link, and those bad feelings float away. Empathy makes the world a better place.

Leptospirosis*

At the time of the flood, the Earth was populated by nephilim. Angels descended from heaven, impregnated mortal women. The women were happy to have partners who weren't cousins. These women would give birth to a race of giants, the Elioud, whom God would ultimately drown for their sins.

The street had been barricaded, but God watched as someone moved the roadblocks in the middle of the night. Then He watched a family of five drive past, into the water. Hours later, emergency vehicles found the truck. Inside were two sinners, their lungs full of silt and brown water. It's been three days since the rain ended.

The lights flicker on, and my alarm clock begins blinking noon. To the rhythm of the flashing red, I fill the kettle with fecal coliform and rat urine, giving the dial a spin to "high." My tastes run exotic, and my bloodlust is legendary, yet I do not seek an infantryman's death. I have done my time in the trenches, as indicated by the blood that oozes from between my gums. The troop Doctor attributed my disease to psychological stress. In keeping with the motif, he called it shell shock. Nowadays, we use new words for that, whispering them in the halls of the drowning VA Hospital, under the noses of forgotten heroes. The kettle screams for morphine, and I add denatured proteins to the coffee grounds. Four minutes later, I push down the plunger, sending little bubbles of air screaming from beneath the press. A couple of scoops of sugar, and a splash of milk help the spirochaetes go down smooth.

The state's infrastructure is in full rebellion. During the night, the parking lot of the Methodist church opens up, a friendly invitation to curious parishioners. Just drive your car into the sinkhole, and the Devil will be on the other side to unlock your door. "Glad you could make it," he says. "Sorry about the weather. We've been having some difficulties with the plumbing." The driver makes a joke about lawyers, and the Devil laughs politely. He's heard that one so many times before. His patience is running thin.

I watch from the window, sipping my bean oil and dead bacteria. I cover my nakedness, and count the onlookers, making bets with myself as to who will be the next to jump. The sun is coming out, and the old ladies are getting excited. They should jump any minute.

Munchausen Syndrome

I'm sorry. I'm not feeling well today. I won't be able to make it in. My throat is really sore, and I've been feeling kind of nauseous.

When I was a child, I succeeded without trying, and that passive success became not just the standard to which I was held, but the standard to which I would hold myself. When it became clear that there was a threshold, a cap to the superiority over my peers, I discovered that I was smart, but no more so than many people I had known for most of my life. By the end of high school, I had to face the reality that I was not spectacular. I was normal.

A fictional mother tells a fictional son that she failed as a mother, and I spend the evening crying. How can I miss degradation this badly? Why do I long for a tangible ailment? Am I white and liberal enough to write out my pent-up sexual expression, and call it closure? Can I sell my story to an independent film studio, eager for more tales of disaffected depressives upset when their parents start dying? How much will they give me? And will I finally be able to afford the ways and means to reprogram three decades of illness?

The Doctor recommends a patch that seeps opium into my flesh. He says, "it will make you normal." Upon leaving his office, I saturate it with butane. I watch the flame change from yellow to blue. The heat will sterilize me, clean me of fear and failures. My disease is real, I keep repeating. If it weren't, would the treatment be as perfectly ineffective?

Peptic Ulcer

In the end, my aunt is to blame. Her fault for feeling chosen, for attending the seminary, for being ordained into the faith of her parents and mine. My mother's best friend looks at her sideways and shakes her head. "Women can't be pastors. No disrespect, but the path of your life is wrong. Your sense of purpose is misplaced. I know this better than anyone." Still, I should lay the blame on the caterers, for choosing their path, for attending whatever school they send aspiring caterers to, for agreeing to the venue, to setting out the tray of grape tomatoes that I devoured by the handful.

Tomatoes are vials of acid, more corrosive than black coffee. In the first weeks of biology 101, you learn about cells, and inside those cells are lysosomes. These are little structures that devour proteins, nucleic acids, whatever detritus threatens to pollute your system. Sometimes scientists call them "suicide sacs," which I find misleading, and suggests that they dissolve themselves in their acid, the same pH as tomatoes. I swallowed half a pound of homicide sacs, declaring open war on my stomach, trying to melt my genome from the inside out. After an hour or so, my nerve endings started screaming.

The first time I experienced heartburn, twisting on the bed of a private school dorm, I thought I was dying. That presumed death was nothing compared to a belly full of acid. Time slowed down as I sweated through my unironed shirt and clip-on tie. As I doubled over, I imagined the newscasts: "Teenager dead of tomato overdose. His blood is now being sold as the 58th variety." My encroaching demise was treated less like the emergency I experienced it as, and more as an inconvenience, making my parents drive me home without sticking around to clean up. I struggled during the ride home, but within an hour, the pain had ended as suddenly as it began. That was the first of the stomach aches. I had invited in a vampire, and I could no longer keep it out.

The Doctor said it was probably a simple disease, one with a comical three-word name that invoked old people shitting in diapers. You could abbreviate if you wanted to make it sound more medical. "It's Bull Shit," I said. "What are the other options?"

"Exocrine pancreatic insufficiency."

"Next."

The Doctor told me about another disease, more dramatic, bloodier, harder to test for. Swallow a gallon of oil well drilling fluid, take some photographs, see what we see. He says it's a waste of time. I'm not bleeding in my stomach.

"How do you know?"

"You'd know."

The acid in the tomatoes pales in comparison to the contents of your stomach, which curdles blood on contact. The terms become less technical in these cases. Hematemesis is close, but too vague for these purposes. Hematochezia only gives part of the story. I don't vomit coffee grounds. I don't shit dark tar. Diagnosis: nervous wreck with a tender tummy.

Here's a lollipop. Now get the fuck out of my office, kid.

Alzheimer's Disease

Dear Dr. Skinner,

I should have reached out sooner, but I seem to only delve into nostalgia when I'm at my most powerless. Someone mentioned my old school in passing, and that was what it took for me to remember you. I realized how much I had to say to you, and before I had assembled my words, I found out just how much you had lost. When I knew you, your wife was the sick one. She had spent twenty years with her own immune system stripping the insulation from her neurons. You were emotional about the books you assigned, but you only cried when you spoke about her. Ten years later, she's the one who answers the phone. She tells me that you are on a puree diet, that you can no longer eat solid foods. How can I expect you to remember a mediocre student from over ten years ago? You can't remember how to chew.

When you're young, you fear losing your genitals. When you're middle-aged, you fear losing your body. When you're old, you fear losing everything about yourself. You and your friends have discussed the different ways you would beat the diagnosis: a handful of pills, a blade in the bathtub, or the simplicity of a loaded revolver. But when it comes, you can't remember your convictions. Your life drains away from you in a widening stream, good memories and bad. If you're lucky, you don't think about your losses. If you're less lucky, you relive those losses everyday.

There has to be something left that we can talk about. There has to be something left in you. How can a brain as complex as yours have the lights turned completely out? When I talk to your wife, we talk about heady concepts, far too intimate for two people who have never met before. We talk about meaning and hope. We talk about faith, but without once using the word "God".

I don't say it, but I think of my favorite pairing: order and chaos. I think of waste. Her muscles, your mind, my security, lost to a pandemonium of absence.

Yours in loss,

M

Beriberi*

My neck is hurting again. If it had been hurting since this morning, I would think it was due to sleeping wrong. This one didn't start until the afternoon, after I'd already written down my latest sorry excuse for a poem. I chalk the pain up to poor posture. In a different journal, I made a list of all the different specialists I need to see: the dentist for my cavities, the ENT for my sleep apnea, the mineralogist for the stones. At the very bottom of the list is the chiropractor.

I imagine him as he's portrayed in the movies, pushing a disc into just the right position, putting his whole weight into it. There's a loud crack, followed by an unimaginable pain that blooms into a new life-affirming analgesia. It only dawns on me later that the problem may not be my bones, but the waterfall of cervical nerves that cascade from my spinal cord. I self-diagnose the problem between my fourth and fifth vertebrae. The nerves there control my diaphragm, my biceps, and my ability to shrug. When I shrug, I feel the pressure push upwards. Like the poem, it points an accusing finger at my brain.

If I was having trouble walking, or felt the need to vomit, it could be an inflammation of the neurons. Symptoms include paralysis. There's a second form of the disease that involves my heart. Vasodilation, peripheral oedema. My socks don't fit well, but I'm not leaking fluids yet. The third form is seen in infants. The fourth, newly discovered and freshly talked about, results in abdominal pain. I flash to my phantom ulcer, and sigh a far too tranquil sigh. There's contentment in old pain, understood and familiar.

The one thing it couldn't be is vitamin deficiency. I pay out the nose for these smoothies that are made with kale and chia seeds and potting soil. Only pirates get scurvy. Only Soviet laborers get pellagra. I don't have a peg leg, or hands hardened by the Gulag. This isn't a writer's curse, a mental block transformed into life, bacterial or viral.

Roughly translated, it reads "I cannot. I cannot." I'm on my knees, palms outstretched, repeating the name of the disease. I cannot. I cannot. I never could.

The Doctor told me a story about his last practice.

At his last practice, he had been greeted warmly by all the staff, and in no time, he felt right at home. He had a wonderful rapport with the secretaries, the transcriptionists, the phlebotomists, and the nurses. But there was another doctor, an older man with fading red in his beard, who distrusted the Doctor. He made it his mission to get the Doctor fired.

One day, the Doctor called out sick, and the Older had to take his patients for the day. One was a young man who had been visiting the practice for pain management. Nothing had effectively managed his pain, and the young man was getting very tired of seeing no progress. The Older told him, "I'll write you a prescription that I guarantee will cure you."

The young man, excited, asked, "Right now?"

The Older shook his head. "First, I need you to do something for me."

The next day, the Doctor came back to work, to find the staff gathered around his personal computer. Two days ago, his wallpaper had been of a fancy car that he had always wanted to buy. Now, it was a picture of a man anally penetrating another man. Some of the staff tried to speak to his character, but the Administrators had seen too much. The Doctor was fired that afternoon.

The young man returned to the Older, nervous about returning to the scene of the crime. However, his desire for pain treatment outweighed his fear of being caught, so again he slipped into the Older's office. "I did what you asked. What do you have for me?"

The Older scribbled on his pad. "I'm writing you a prescription for colloidal silver. Thirty milligrams. Take them with a meal."

Serotonin Syndrome

There was once a girl named Libby Zion. She was a freshman at a college in Vermont, and she couldn't handle the college experience on her own. She was taking an antidepressant, a bright orange pill that would have looked completely at home in a grocery store gumball machine. Her orange pill was an MAOI, a type of drug that had begun to fall out of favor with the medical establishment.

In March, Libby began to show flu-like symptoms, and after a couple of days, she was checked into the hospital for observation. Treatment for the flu consists of bed rest, fluids, and in particularly serious cases, antiviral medication. Her doctors noticed that she had a noticeable tic, and to quell it, they administered pethidine. Pethidine is a synthetic opioid, considered a Schedule II drug alongside cocaine and PCP.

Libby's condition worsened, and the doctor had her restrained. They gave her Haldol. Her temperature spiked to 107 degrees, and she suffered a cardiac arrest. She did not wake up.

My medication is an SNRI, which means it inhibits different chemical processes than the deadly orange pills. They give mine to elderly women for the treatment of menopause. Libby would only be turning fifty this year, so she should be safe.

On the list of uncommon side effects, I find some gems: hypomania, epistaxis, depersonalization. Rare side effect: a disease where my skin will rot off my body. I make the mistake of searching for images, and Google presents me a wall of living corpses. The video I watch opens with a commercial for a plaque psoriasis treatment. A thin woman with long brown hair bemoans the scaly skin that make her self-conscious about wearing shorts. After five seconds, she's replaced by another young brunette. This one takes a Zantac, and ends up with a feeding tube, and her flesh weeping pus into a hospital bed.

When I read about her fingernails falling off, mine go into my mouth. I nervously chew, tasting grit and butane, before remembering that I have another medication for anxiety. Among its rare side effects: thrombocytopenia, ataxia, psychosis, rage. It may cause depression. It may increase the risk of suicide. The Doctor recommends I only take it as needed, such as when I'm depressed or feel at risk of suicide. The Doctor doesn't understand irony. I don't think they teach it at medical school. I wouldn't know.

Anton-Babinski Syndrome*

For my father

Things are great. Why do you ask?

This past weekend was just like any other. I knew what to expect. She had been leaving me lovesick texts, finding new words to describe how she missed me. When I showed up that evening, she greeted me with a smile, with adoration in her eyes. Just by that immediate glance, I could tell that despite all the years, despite the arguments and the moments of isolation, despite those times when it might have seemed like we couldn't stand each other, she still loved me just as much as she did on the day that we got married.

I have a pile of photos, snapshots saved from our vacations: kissing beneath the Eiffel Tower, smashing wedding cake into each other's faces...oh, here we go. It's that time we got lost in downtown Atlanta. I'm surprised I haven't told you about that one before. It was one of those once in a lifetime experiences that you just keep taking photographs of, because you feel that if you ever stop, somehow that moment might slip out of your mind.

Well, obviously, we're not both in the pictures. Someone had to take them, and the week prior she had a bad experience with her hair stylist, and despite all my assurances that she still looked beautiful, she thought it made her look like a rabid chicken. It's doubly funny, because chickens can't get rabies. They can actually carry the disease, but they never exhibit any symptoms, and they almost always recover completely. Sorry, I'm getting off topic, but I just found that really funny.

The photos you're referring to are taken inside, away from any landmarks. You don't honestly believe that we just sat around posing in front of the Coke Museum or the Tabernacle? The hotel we stayed at must use a similar contractor to the ones who built our apartment. That's why you're getting confused. It's alright. It could happen to anybody. Just keep looking, you'll find the pictures I'm talking about.

Of course, everything's fine. I'm not sure why you feel you have to keep asking. I told you, nothing has changed. It was only seven days, how much can our lives really change in that period, truth be told?

That's just from the cat. It doesn't look that bad. I'm being relative, of course. The cat's scratched me much worse than that in the past. He gets excited to jump in my lap, and he puts his front paws on my arms, and if he loses balance, he doesn't really understand the etiquette which you're trying to apply to him. He's just a dumb fucking cat, and he gave me a dumb fucking scratch. Fine, he gave me a dumb fucking cut. Fine, he gave me five distinct fucking cuts lined up in a perfect row. Yes, I saw it happen.

Yes, she still loves me.

Yes, she wants to be with me.

No, my illness hasn't hurt us.

No, her illness hasn't risen to meet it.

No, she's still part of the family.

Yes, you should keep writing her checks.

Yes, she believes in our future.

Yes, I believe in a future.

Yes, our lives will be spent together.

Why do you keep asking these questions?

I'm not blind, everything is just fine. I'm not blind.

I'm not.

Cancer of the Pancreas

For my mother

You deserved better.

When I sat by your bedside at the hospital, I wanted to say that I was sorry. At the time, I didn't know what I was sorry for, but a year out, I might finally be lucid enough to understand my intentions.

I'm sorry that your body betrayed you. I'm sorry that when your metabolism turned on you, like it had on both of your sisters, that it chose the worst of the prospective paths. I'm sorry the cells in your pancreas didn't have the common decency to stop growing. Those cells were all wrong, and your body cast them out into your organ systems, perhaps in a misguided attempt to find the proper place for them.

I'm sorry I didn't read about dysplastic nevus syndrome.

I'm sorry I didn't seek out a gene map for CDKN2A.

I'm sorry I didn't recommend gene therapy.

I'm sorry I never became knowledgeable enough to diagnose my family.

I'm sorry I never became a Doctor.

I'm sorry that you had the demons that you had, though I understand why I never knew about all of them. I'm not sure what I could have done, anyway. Your best friend told me I have to let go of the past, to not let anger rule me. I've been told that it would tarnish your memory. I feel it would be an insult to your memory if I weren't angry. I'll spend the next year hanging up on your friend. If I could reach past your lifeless eyes and drag those cruelties out by the root, I would.

I'm sorry if my demons, inescapable and yet somehow reliable, pushed me further away than I realized. Our unhappiness was a link that neither of us wanted to acknowledge. It pitted us against each other, and as my hindsight attempts to rewrite history, my memories give way to elaborate fantasies of us bonding over these complexities. We're smiling, laughing, and joking at the expense of ourselves, and our disease.

I'm sorry I can't breathe life into the photo albums. Every day, these images grow less defined, and though it hasn't been a full year, I fear losing you completely. I fear waking up one day, and looking at the picture of me outside the college's student union, still a gangly teenager with a bad haircut and a fondness for Mello Yello, and wondering who is that woman? Who is that woman, familiar enough with me, to rest her head on my shoulder? The look on my face is one of embarrassment, yet I still let her into my personal space, where she smiles with amusement, maybe even pride.

I'm sorry that now, this is all I can give you. I've written for a year, filling up digital pages with thousands of words that amount to such a small percentage of available data. Printed out, these pages could wallpaper my apartment and your tomb. All I have are these words, brought forth from some place deep inside of me, intermingled with my tissues. More malignant than benign.

The stain exhales. And life goes back to zero.

•

Anton-Babinski Syndrome - a condition where blind people deny being blind

Aphasia - loss of ability to understand or express speech, caused by brain damage

Argyria - a condition caused by inappropriate exposure to chemical compounds of silver

Beriberi - malnutrition produced by an inadequate amount of Vitamin B-1 in the diet

Couvade Syndrome - sympathetic pregnancy

Kwashiorkor - malnutrition produced by a severely inadequate amount of protein in the diet

Leptospirosis - a bacterial disease spread through the urine of infected animals

Psittacosis - a zoonotic infectious disease caused by a bacterium contracted from infected birds

Teratoma - a tumor that may contain several types of body tissue, including hair, eyes, and teeth;

Literal definition: "monster tumor"

Matthew O'Leary grew up and lives in Columbia, South Carolina. He has had work featured in *Gravel* magazine, *Birds Piled Loosely*, and *Fall Lines*. If you enjoy this book, buy him a cup of coffee. If you don't, buy him a cup of tea. He hates tea. Find more of his work at matthewoleary.wordpress.com.

Muddy Ford Press

is a boutique publishing house working hand-in-hand with South Carolina authors to share and celebrate the rich stores of literary talent found in our state.

For more information go to

MuddyFordPress.com.

The author and his mother

www.ingramcontent.com/pod-product-compliance
Lightning Source LLC
Chambersburg PA
CBHW071842190726
48292CB00005B/1883